Thirty Views of a Changing World

haiku and photos by

Ellen Girardeau Kempler

Finishing Line Press
Georgetown, Kentucky

Thirty Views of a Changing World

Copyright © 2017 by Ellen Girardeau Kempler
ISBN 978-1-63534-367-0 First Edition
All rights reserved under International and Pan-American Copyright Conventions.
No part of this book may be reproduced in any manner whatsoever without written permission from the publisher, except in the case of brief quotations embodied in critical articles and reviews.

ACKNOWLEDGMENTS

Thanks to my husband, Roger Kempler, for his support, encouragement and adventurous spirit; to my daughters, Holly and Alex, for their inspiration; and to my friends and extended family, for cheering me on. I love you all.

This book is dedicated to the world's scientists, environmentalists, leaders and others who continue to work for global peace, climate action and social justice.

Publisher: Leah Maines

Editor: Christen Kincaid

Cover Art: *Sunrise over Mount Fuji* by Ellen Girardeau Kempler, September 2016

Additional Photos: Ellen Girardeau Kempler, 2016-2017

Author Photo: Holly Nicole Kempler, Mont Saint-Michel, France, June 2015

Cover Design: Elizabeth Maines McCleavy

Printed in the USA on acid-free paper.
Order online: www.finishinglinepress.com
also available on amazon.com

Author inquiries and mail orders:
Finishing Line Press
P. O. Box 1626
Georgetown, Kentucky 40324
U. S. A.

Table of Contents

1	View Rock
2	Laguna Beach Goats
3	Saint Florian
4	Eucalyptus Sunburst
5	Pothole Heart
6	Pomegranate
7	Mossy Rocks
8	Crystal Cove Hike
9	Split-Rock Heart
10	Bommer Ridge Trail
11	Bamboo Forest
12	Monarch
13	Yucca Bouquet
14	Old Fence
15	Golden Waterfall
16	SoCal Heat
17	Yosemite Falls Rainbow
18	Santa Ana Sunset
19	Thunder Moon
20	Blue Wall
21	Sunrise, Moonset
22	Stand Up Paddlers
23	Low Tide Treasure
24	Tokyo Subway
25	Torii Tunnel
26	Lava Field, Moss
27	Hiroshima Memorial
28	A-Bomb Dome
29	Water Glacier Hike
30	Mount Fuji Sunrise

Author's Note: I took all photos in Laguna Beach, California, with the exception of 11, 15, 16, 17 and 24-30. Photo 11 was taken at Arashiyama, outside Kyoto, Japan; 15 at Gullfoss, along Iceland's Golden Circle; 16, at California State University, Fullerton; 17, in Yosemite National Park, California; 24 and 25, in Japan; 26, at Eldhraun Lava Field, Iceland; 27 and 28, at the Hiroshima Memorial Peace Park, Japan; 29, at Vatnajökull, southern Iceland; and 30, at Lake Ashinoko, Japan.

Introduction

In January 2016 I made a resolution to take at least one photo and write an accompanying haiku every day. Since then, no matter how many distractions the world spins my way, I always find time to look, focus, photograph, write and refine these moments into finished reflections.

Most of the image/haiku views in this book appeared online under my Instagram alias, @placepoet. The title is a reference to "Thirty-Six Views of Mount Fuji," the classic woodprint series by Edo-era Japanese artist Hokusai. "Changing world" refers to climate change and other world-altering pressures facing us today. I took most photos near home in southern California, with a few from trips to Iceland and Japan.

In choosing my subjects, I tried to follow the advice of haiku master Matsuo Bashō in *The Narrow Road to the Deep North* (copyright Nobuyuki Yuasa, 1966; published in English by Penguin Books), "Go to the pine if you want to learn about the pine, or to the bamboo if you want to learn about the bamboo. And in doing so, you must leave your subjective preoccupation with yourself."

By sharing these reflections as widely as possible on digital platforms, I hope to inspire others to action. As former *Poetry Magazine* Editor Christian Wiman wrote, "...in the end we go to poetry for one reason, so that we might more fully inhabit our lives and the world in which we live them, and that if we more fully inhabit these things, we might be less apt to destroy both."

From view rock, the fire-
season hits too close
to home. Dry. Dry. Dry.

The firefighting herd
eats any plant, dead or alive.
No fuel left for fire.

Patron saint of fire-
fighters, keep us safe from wild
winds carrying sparks.

Sunburst hangs like ripe
fruit, too bright to pick. Burning
eucalyptus crowns.

First fall rain fills my
thirsty heart with hope for
a wet, green winter.

Blessing from a drought-
tested garden: A single
hail-bright pomegranate.

A green surprise for
thirsty eyes: water, water
still no drop to drink.

No trail here. We skirt
the waves, staying cool below
the hot, thirsty hills.

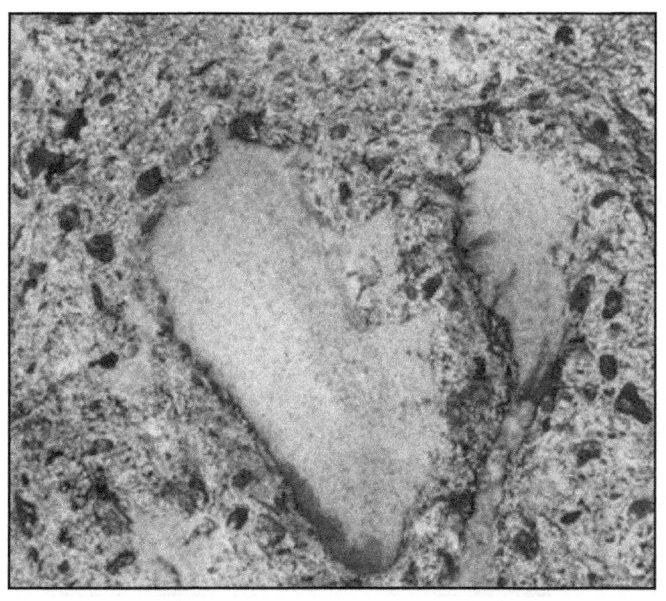

Split-rock heart, open
to breaking waves, wind, sand, salt
rising ocean tides.

On these sun-scorched trails
you can hike for miles and miles.
Always pack water.

Forest of bamboo,
a gray-green haze leading up
toward pure, white light.

Monarch in the street:
Did you fly from two doors down,
my milkweed hostel?

A spiky yucca
bouquet, a welcome gift at
summer's bleakest time.

Windows into time
ravages of termites, moss
and rot. Dust to dust.

Iron air, copper
cliffs, green cascades carry time's
tarnish through eons.

Southern California
fall: hot shock of pink against
bright sky. Silk floss tree.

At 7 a.m. we
find the pot of gold. Tourists
still asleep. Rainbow.

Santa Ana dusk.
Wild winds paint air pollution
on the dusty sky.

No rain headed here
yet the full Thunder Moon still
shines through bone-dry oaks.

Against tides, concrete
cannot stand. Waves and water
will conquer coastline.

Morning commute, moon
and sun in transit, passing
the bright horizon.

Gray, glassy ocean
mirrors mourning. Don't drown, World.
Paddle together.

With waves like dust brooms
tides sweep shells, kelp, rock into
tourist temptations.

Silent geisha watch
but can't help navigate.
Born before Google.

In this forest, red
torii gates light the tunnel
trail. No solitude.

Laki's fury left
a lava field moss can't hide.
Volcanoes rage here.

The cenotaph holds
names of Hiroshima dead.
Shelter them in peace.

At dusk Genbaku
Dome glows with unnatural
light. Silent witness.

Dying glacier
lit with faint sapphire ghost-light:
rare and precious view.

Lake-mirror reflects
a faraway Fuji, no
sign of time-worn trails.

Ellen Girardeau Kempler is an award-winning nonfiction writer and poet. After a 25-year career in nonprofit communications, a layoff inspired her to enroll in a poetry workshop in Ireland and launch her website, Gold Boat Journeys (Creative Cultural Travel). Since then, she has organized trips around events such as writers' conferences, book and music festivals and literary anniversaries and holidays. An active environmentalist, she champions sustainable, culturally immersive, car-free travel. In the past few years, her wanderings have taken her to Chile, Israel, Jordan, Iceland, Germany, West Africa, France, Ireland, Canada, Costa Rica, Mexico, Japan and around the U.S.

Her poems have been published in *Cargo Literary, Gold Man Review; Phoenix Rising Review, Orbis International Poetry Quarterly, Spectrum* and a number of other small presses. They have also been shortlisted for the Tom Howard and Margaret Reid Poetry Award, the Tucson Festival of Books Literary Prize and Fish Poetry Prize, and have won three first-place awards and one second-place award in the annual Laguna Beach Library Poetry Contest. In 2016 one of her poems won Ireland's Blackwater International Poetry Prize. Her travel writing, essays, opinion pieces and feature articles have appeared in *The Atlantic, L.A. Times, Christian Science Monitor, Huffington Post, Culture Trip, Transitions Abroad, Westways* and numerous other publications.

Based in Laguna Beach, California, she enjoys hiking, gardening, baking, reading and volunteering for theaters and other community groups. She believes in poetry's power to reach hearts, change minds and move people to action. *Thirty Views of a Changing World* is her first book.

www.ingramcontent.com/pod-product-compliance
Lightning Source LLC
LaVergne TN
LVHW041509070426
835507LV00012B/1449